Looking at Paintings

Dancers

Isadora Duncan,
Antoine Bourdelle, Pen and ink, 1909

LOOKING AT PAINTINGS

Dancers

Peggy Roalf

Series Editor
Jacques Lowe

Designer
Amy Hill

Belitha Press
London

A
JACQUES LOWE
VISUAL ARTS PROJECTS
BOOK

Text © 1992 by Jacques Lowe Visual Arts Projects Inc.
A Jacques Lowe Visual Arts Projects Book

Printed in Italy

First published in the United States by Hyperion Books for Children

First published in the United Kingdom in 1994 by
Belitha Press Ltd
31 Newington Green, London N16 9PU

Cataloguing-in-print data available from the British Library

ISBN 1 85561 355 7

Original design concept by Amy Hill
UK editor: Kate Scarborough

Contents

Introduction

LOOKING AT PAINTINGS is a series of books about understanding what great artists see when they paint. Painters have been attracted to the movement and the excitement of dance for more than 2,000 years. By looking at many paintings of this one subject, we see how these artists have brought their personal vision of dancers to life, using talent and imagination.

Painters are creative explorers. They use their feelings about the world around them to decide what to paint and how to use their materials. Gifted artists can look at something as simple as a playground dance and create a unique painting with light, colour and movement. With their singular power of observation, they can find something unusual in everything they see and often create revolutionary painting techniques to express their points of view.

We will see that Henri Matisse revealed the powerful energy in a circle dance by using bold lines and three brilliant colours in *The Dance* (page 37). Henri de Toulouse-Lautrec watched a graceful figure and captured pure movement with a luminous swirl of colour, in *Loie Fuller in the Dance of the Veils at the Folies-Bergères* (page 33). Georges Seurat created a new way of painting with thousands of flickering little dots in *The Can-Can* (page 35).

Artists transform what they see into magical images that take us on a journey to earlier times and to distant places. You can learn to observe the world around you and use your imagination to see things like a painter.

Note: words in **bold** are explained in the glossary on page 46.

MAENAD WITH STAFF AND TAMBOURINE, about 60 B.C.
Unknown Roman Artist, **fresco** (detail)

Rich people lived like kings in ancient Rome. They built beautiful villas with marble halls and swimming pools and gave big parties. They hired artists to paint pictures of their gods and goddesses on the walls of these villas. For five days every spring, the Romans stopped working to celebrate the festival of Dionysus, the god of wine. Paintings of Dionysus and his followers, who were called maenads, have been found in a villa near Pompeii. In A.D. 79, the volcano Mount Vesuvius erupted and buried the city of Pompeii under lava. The lava sealed in everything, so many villas and their paintings were saved from the destruction of time.

Worshippers of Dionysus

Maenads were always pictured carrying ivy-topped staffs and tambourines. They worshipped Dionysus with music and wild dancing in the mountain forests. The maenad in this painting seems to float in the air. Even so, the artist painted with great feeling, using delicate colours and shading to represent the **transparency** of the dancer's robe floating on the wind as she steps along. The background was painted black so that the maenad would look very bright. The Roman painter created this sharp contrast to focus our attention on the dancer's beauty.

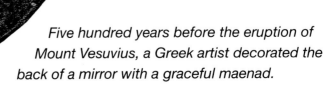

Five hundred years before the eruption of Mount Vesuvius, a Greek artist decorated the back of a mirror with a graceful maenad.

9

RECEPTION AT THE COURT OF SHAH TAHMASP,
early 17th century
Unknown Persian Artist, fresco (detail)

Shah Tahmasp, a king of Persia, knew how to give a party. He put on a lavish feast when Prince Humayūn of India came to visit, and this is the scene pictured in this wall painting. Fresco is an ancient method of painting with pure colour directly on to a wet plaster wall. When the paint and plaster dry, they become one material instead of one material on top of another (as in **oil paints** and **canvas**). For this reason, we can look at a fresco from any angle and not be distracted by a shiny surface. And since the picture becomes part of the **architecture**, artists consider fresco to be the ideal method for wall painting.

The wealth of the court

The artist who created this fresco put many details into the painting to show great luxury, wealth and power. Mouth-watering fruits spill out of richly patterned bowls. The shah watches over the festivities from a platform, wearing a turban studded with feathers and precious gems. Palace guards stand by to protect their king, and graceful dancers entertain.

Shah Abbas, Tahmasp's successor, built the **Chihil Sitin** for official receptions. He decorated the walls with this fresco to honour Tahmasp and to remind visitors of the splendour of his own court.

The detailed portraits of this dancer and the one above create a strong focus in the fresco.

THE WEDDING DANCE, about 1566
Pieter Brueghel the Elder, Flemish (1525/30–1569), oil on panel, 118 x 155 cm

More than four hundred years ago, when this picture was painted, farmers worked from dawn to dusk to make a living. At that time political, religious and civil wars raged in Europe. Worn out by hard labour and the fear of war, the peasants had few reasons to celebrate. So when there was a wedding, the entire village turned out for a party. Pieter Brueghel painted one such wedding in full swing.

A crowded party

There are more than one hundred people in this scene—dancing, drinking, playing tag and gossiping. Brueghel made all these activities visible, using colour to lead our eyes, little by little, from the bottom of the picture to the top. Patches of red dance from right to left to right and back.

Earth colours

If Brueghel had used too much red paint, the activities would have all blended together. So he also used light colours. Brueghel painted blouses and jackets in golden earthy colours. He gave the same pale greenish colour of the ground to the men's **britches**, the tunics and the aprons. Brueghel painted these people of the earth with the colours of the earth.

But where is the bride? Look carefully and find the only woman who is not wearing a handkerchief on her head.

Brueghel painted each dancer's clothing with individual style, as seen in this detail.

PEASANTS' DANCE, 1636/40
Peter Paul Rubens, Flemish (1577–1640), oil on panel, 71 x 104 cm

Peter Paul Rubens is known as 'the prince of painters' because he painted the energy of life into his work. He created majestic portraits of princes and bankers, huge pictures of historical events and religious scenes for cathedrals. The archduke and archduchess who ruled the Low Countries (now known as the Netherlands) noticed his great talent and employed him to be their official painter.

Painting for himself

After thirty years of creating large-scale works for important people, Rubens felt he deserved some time to paint for his own enjoyment. He moved to a country house and spent time outside, sketching the natural world and local farmers.

Inspired by the vision of Pieter Brueghel (page 12), Rubens painted his own view of a peasant dance in his own particular style. The peasants dance in a zigzag line that gives a feeling of movement to the picture. Each face is an individual portrait, which draws the viewer into the scene. He painted the dancers' skin using a see-through **glaze** on top of **opaque** paint. Rubens' technique allowed the colours underneath to shine through. The peasants' skin seems to glow with a light that shines from within.

In this detail, Rubens shows that hands can be as expressive as faces. He also contrasts a pretty face with rough working hands.

14

CARNIVAL SCENE, about 1756
Giovanni Domenico Tiepolo, Italian (1727–1804)
oil on canvas, 74 x 118 cm

If somebody said to us, 'Tell me the difference between looking at something and seeing something', we might say that there is no difference. And we would be absolutely wrong.

Giovanni Domenico Tiepolo grew up learning to see every detail of his surroundings from his father, who was a famous painter named Giovanni Battista Tiepolo. Domenico could look at a view and see what was in front of him as one big picture or focus in on small parts of the scene.

Domenico's ability to observe the world around him and paint a vivid and imaginative picture of it made him a popular artist.

The carnival

Domenico brought an afternoon party in the country to life with action and detail. Carnivals were often held at his family's villa near Venice. In this scene, two dancers perform in the foreground, while actors in masks and tall hats await their turn. We can easily tell who the guests are because their clothes are plainer than those of the dancers and actors.

Domenico made this painting of the party, the lively dance and the wonderful silky costumes so life-like that we can really tell what it was like to be a wealthy Venetian in the 1750s.

Another Italian artist, Pinelli, shows the costumes worn by dancers one hundred years later.

16

BUGAKU DANCE, about 1720
Hanabusa Itchō, Japanese (1652–1724), ink and **water-colour** on **gold leaf**,
181 x 444 cm

Hanabusa Itchō lived in Japan at a time of peace and prosperity, when wealthy merchants and military rulers spent great sums to decorate their mansions. These buildings had huge rooms that were dark and draughty. Instead of walls to separate rooms, large moveable screens were used to divide the space.

The painter of this screen was inspired by the Japanese art of fabric design.

The Bugaku

The figures in the picture are painted on to a four-and-a-half-metre-wide screen which illustrates an ancient dance called Bugaku; they prowl, pounce and stamp their feet to the music of wooden flutes and drums. Itchō used brilliantly-coloured **inks** and water-colours for the figures. He created the painting for a very wealthy person, so he could afford to put a film of real gold all over the background. The light that bounced off the shiny surface would have brightened up the room.

Like other great Japanese artists, Itchō found beauty in the spaces between figures. He shaped the golden areas around the dancers and made them just as interesting as the costumes.

Itchō modelled his designs on a similar screen painted forty five years earlier by his teacher, Kano Yasunobu. And Yasunobu got his idea by looking at a painting created one hundred years before. Each painter used the work of another artist as a starting point, then made his own original version of the classic dance.

OBERON, TITANIA AND PUCK WITH FAIRIES, DANCING, 1785
William Blake, English (1757–1827), water-colour on paper, 47 x 66 cm

William Blake was a great poet as well as a painter. He created this water-colour to illustrate a play called *A Midsummer Night's Dream*, which was written in the sixteenth century by another great poet, William Shakespeare.

The play tells the story of two pairs of lovers who are in love with the wrong partners. Oberon, king of the fairies, ordered his chief spirit, the mischievous Puck, to sprinkle nectar from an enchanted flower into the men's eyes while they slept. On waking, each falls in love with the first person he sees. This leads to all sorts of problems! After all the confusion is sorted out, Oberon, Queen Titania and their followers celebrate the lovers' rightful weddings. As the play ends, the fairies dance and sing before disappearing.

The movements of dancers in a circle fascinated Nicholas Poussin (1593–1665).

Painting mystery

William Blake painted this last scene with water-colours. He created velvety deep tones for the mysterious night-time forest by painting on many layers of colour. The water-colour paint is transparent, so the colours underneath shine through. For the figures, Blake used only a few layers of pale, luminous colour, and then applied some darker touches of paint for the shadows. He used the magical qualities of water-colour to express the enchantment of a midsummer night.

BULL DANCE, MANDAN O-KEE-PA CEREMONY, 1832
George Catlin, American (1796–1872), oil on canvas, 61 x 70 cm

George Catlin had a personal mission. He visited the Great Plains Indians before photography was widely used and painted pictures of their customs to create a unique record. He believed that their native way of life would be destroyed by white explorers and fur traders who brought a different culture to the tribes.

Catlin often travelled alone through the wild and dangerous western states, carrying his painting supplies on his back. He made friends with the chiefs who invited him to live in their villages.

Ceremonial dance

The Bull Dance was part of the most important Mandan ceremony. Eight braves wearing buffalo skins with willow branches tied to their backs and four others with painted bodies and towering head-dresses perform the dance. They ask their god, the Great Spirit, to bring the tribe success in hunting. Catlin painted this view from the top of one of the buffalo-hide lodges to give us a bird's-eye view of the ceremony.

Catlin wanted to show the unspoiled nature of the native Americans, so he used what is known as a '**primitive**' style of painting. He made the shapes simpler than they really were, using bold, almost child-like patches of colour.

The Plains Indians believed that magical powers enabled George Catlin to paint a likeness of their chief.

A SUMMER NIGHT, 1890
Winslow Homer, American (1836–1910), oil on canvas, 74 x 99 cm

Imagine the most glorious night of summer. The full moon rises so high you have to crane your necks to see it. Everybody goes out to watch the brilliant moonlight casting shadows of clouds on to the rolling surf. The boys crowd on to the rocks and sing, as two girls whirl about on the porch. Summer evenings like this were common at Winslow Homer's home in Maine, USA, and here he captured the radiant light in *A Summer Night*.

Light and shadow

If you look closely, you can see that Homer put more than one kind of light into this picture. The moonlight behind the people on the rocks make them look like **silhouettes**. You have to imagine that bright lights from the house cast the long shadows of the dancers on to the porch. In the distance, a red lighthouse beam glimmers on the horizon. Homer used the contrast of warm, bright light and deep cool shadows to recreate the mood of the most perfect summer night by the sea.

Studio work

Winslow Homer's studio sat on a cliff above the fierce Atlantic Ocean. He made a **charcoal** drawing of this night scene on the spot to catch the effects of different kinds of light. Later, in his studio on the beach, he asked two neighbours to pose for the dance. He studied his drawings and combined all his ideas to create this large painting that he had originally called 'Buffalo Gals'.

THE DANCE CLASS, 1876
Edgar Degas, French (1834–1917), oil on canvas, 84 x 74 cm

The lesson seems endless and the teacher demands one more try from the ballerina in the middle. The girl with the green bow impatiently flutters her fan, the one next to her yawns and scratches. Even the little dog under the piano looks bored.

Edgar Degas painted an ordinary moment in these dancers' lives with affection. He admired the efforts they made to perfect their movements. And the careful repetition of the dance lessons gave him the opportunity to capture their motion in his drawings.

Painting from memory

In his studio, Degas painted this large picture using his memory and sketches to recreate a classroom scene. The steady gaze of the dance master, the great mirror in the centre and the red ribbons and fan of the first dancer focus our attention on the ballerina in the middle. The high ceiling of the classroom helps us to realize the importance of this moment. Degas painted a liquid light that bathes the figures in even tones, but he added shadows on the dancers in front to lead our eyes into the action of the painting. By simplifying the details of the dancers' faces and costumes, he helps us feel the nervous energy of the entire group.

*Degas used ink and **gouache** to create this study for the painting opposite.*

TWO DANCERS ON THE STAGE, 1874
Edgar Degas, French (1834–1917), oil on canvas, 61 x 45 cm

We are late for the theatre! The curtain had gone up! As we scurry in the dark to our seats, wondering what we've missed, we glimpse two dancers on the stage.

This painting looks as if it was quickly dashed off to preserve a memory—like a snapshot. The dancer on the right hand side is cut off by one edge of the painting; on the left hand side, the tutu of a third ballerina pokes into the scene.

Influenced by photography

Edgar Degas was fascinated by photography. He especially liked the way photos stop motion and freeze it forever in time. Such pictures were taken in a hurry and the figures were often cut off at the edges. Degas knew that things were happening beyond the margins of the photo, and this made the photo real. He used the same approach in this picture.

Degas gave us a bird's-eye view of the stage from high up in the theatre. He shortened, or telescoped, the distance between his seat and the performance, putting us right into the action. The costumes of the dancers gleam under the lights and the dark back-ground makes the ballerinas stand out even more.

With a few charcoal lines, Degas captured a young dancer's posture.

28

DANCING AT THE MOULIN DE LA GALETTE, 1876
Pierre-Auguste Renoir, French (1841–1919), oil on canvas, 128 x 173 cm

When Renoir was an art student, he said to his teacher, 'I only want to paint things that I really enjoy.' He meant what he said, so his paintings invite us to enter his personal world, where beauty and pleasure are the most important things.

The Moulin de la Galette was a cafe with a garden where people met for Sunday afternoon dances. In this painting, Renoir included his artist friend and the young women who worked nearby. These were people Renoir knew well, and he made them look carefree and relaxed. The friends posed in Renoir's own garden, which had the same kind of dappled light as the cafe garden.

Renoir painted colour glazed over dark areas to create the sparkling effect of sunlight.

Sunlight

Renoir bathed the scene with sunlight sparkling through the trees; the areas of light are filled with colour. He painted details in the foreground figures to separate them from the background—dresses with lace and velvet ribbons, hats and hair-styles, and the men's starched collars. But he painted these details using films of colour over colour, not with outlines and shading. With quick dashes of paint, Renoir suggests that there is a crowd in the background, completing the festive scene.

LOIE FULLER IN THE DANCE OF THE VEILS AT THE FOLIES-BERGERES, 1898
Henri de Toulouse-Lautrec, French (1864–1901), oil on cardboard

*H*enri de Toulouse-Lautrec had a passion for sketching. When he was a child, he drew everywhere—in his school notebooks and even in the margins of his dictionary.

Toulouse-Lautrec went to the theatre almost every evening and sketched the dancers and actors. He created theatrical posters and illustrations for magazines, as well as paintings to hang on the wall.

The artist was enchanted by Loie Fuller, an American entertainer who created the illusion of dance by standing almost still under the brilliant stage lights and waving her long veils of silky material with sticks. With just a few fluid strokes of paint, Toulouse-Lautrec captured the unusual effect of this startling performance.

A new technique
Toulouse-Lautrec used a special trick to make this oil paint look like **pastel**. He put the paint on **blotting paper** to soak out most of the oil, then thinned it with **turpentine**. Because he had removed so much oil, the paint dried quickly and colours had great intensity. The brown cardboard on which he often painted absorbed the colours, adding to the chalk-like quality.

In a quick sketchbook drawing Toulouse-Lautrec captured the great strength of a dancer's legs.

THE CAN-CAN, 1889-90

Georges Seurat, French (1859–1891), oil on canvas, 166 x 136 cm

In France, the last decade of the nineteenth century was filled with laughter and cheer to celebrate a period of prosperity after a war that had nearly ruined the country. There was a feeling of optimism about the twentieth century: the **Industrial Revolution** allowed an easier life for most people and they had more time for fun.

Georges Seurat was inspired by progress and technology, and he developed a 'scientific approach' for expressing feelings with colours: red, yellow and orange meant happiness; brown and grey were for sadness; lavender and blue were for peace.

Dots of colour

Seurat loved Parisian night-life. He painted a dazzling performance of the can-can using dots of colour and simple shapes to express a feeling of fun. Everything about the way he painted this high-kicking dance created motion—the amused expressions of the performers, the steep angle of the bass violin and the dancers' legs, and the upward glance and raised arm of the conductor. Seurat dabbed on the colours in soft little blobs, and he put orange dots over all the bright areas to create a shimmering glow of light.

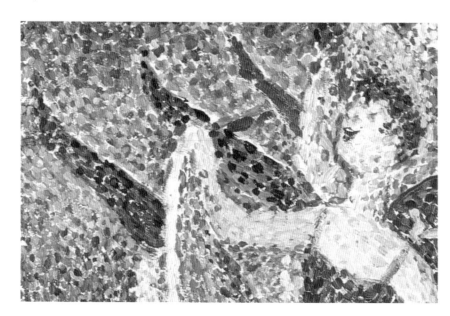

In this detail, we can see how Seurat painted orange dots everywhere, even in the shadows.

35

THE DANCE, 1909
Henri Matisse, French (1869–1954), oil on canvas, 270 x 360 cm

*a*n avalanche of colours has no force,' said Henri Matisse. So he used only three strong colours to show the joy of dancing. He used a bright blue for the sky, the greenest of greens for the grass, and a glowing pink for the figures. We feel the energy of the dance in the bold shapes, rhythmic lines and brilliant colours. Matisse believed that to show the true spirit of an event, you had to throw away every mental picture you had of the subject. And this is what he did by using just a few colours and almost no detail.

Rhythmic movement

The dancers whirl in a ring. Matisse interrupted the circle of arms and created two different rhythms—the figures on the left are graceful and soaring, the ones on the right are angular and awkward. He drew the dancers with bold lines and let the edges of the painting cut into the scene. Matisse liked Japanese painting, so he used the idea of making spaces between the figures important, just as Itchō had done with the Bugaku dancers (page 19).

Matisse also made a charcoal study for The Dance *but changed the form and position of the figures as he drew.*

CITY ACTIVITIES WITH DANCE HALL, 1930
Thomas Hart Benton, American (1889–1975), **tempera** on wood, 230 x 336 cm

Thomas Hart Benton moved from Indiana to New York City, USA, when he decided to be an artist. He wanted to show how ordinary people shaped great events, so he painted **murals** for city buildings—enormous paintings that would be seen by people going to work.

For this mural, Benton travelled through the United States making hundreds of sketches of people in everyday situations, such as making steel, harvesting wheat and having fun. Using these, he created a 29-metre-long painting, *America Today*.

In this section, four couples dance to jazz music; their motion symbolizes the frantic fun-loving style of the **Roaring Twenties**.

Separating scenes
Benton separated the many different events from each other by painting with colours that contrast: red and brown next to green and lavender. He also added streamlined silvery frames to lead our eyes from one story to another across the length of the painting.

Benton separated the scenes in his mural by using contrasting colours and silvery frames.

DANCING IN COLOMBIA, 1980
Fernando Botero, Colombian (born 1932), oil on canvas, 185 x 227 cm

Fernando Botero was born in Colombia, South America, where the enormous Andes Mountains tower over villages and make the houses seem smaller than they really are. Maybe that is why Botero exaggerates the shapes and sizes of the people he paints.

The first thing we notice in this painting is the great difference between the subjects: the towering size of the jazz players and the tiny dancers; the still pose and blank expression of the musicians and the energy of the couple. The dull colours of the men's clothing makes the red in the ties and women's clothing seem brighter than it actually is. The band is playing, but the stringed instruments have no strings and the woodwinds no keys.

Botero painted the colours smoothly on to the canvas, leaving no brush marks on its surface. He used many small details to create a 'frame' around the painting: bare light bulbs above, cigarette butts and apples on the floor, and a red curtain. This frame squeezes the figures into the crowded room and lets us really feel the atmosphere of a noisy party.

In this detail, the missing strings on the guitar and the facial expressions of the musicians are clues to Botero's sense of humour.

OPEN-AIR DANCING IN FLORIDA—1925 (1985)
Oscar de Mejo, American (born in Italy, 1911), **acrylic** on canvas, 70 x 85 cm

Sometimes we have a dream so wonderful we believe it is real. We struggle to stay asleep and keep dreaming. The man who painted this scene gives us a dream from his own childhood. When he lived with his family in Italy, Oscar de Mejo saw a photograph of a party in Florida, and it stuck in his mind. The photo reminded him of American jazz, his favourite music. He painted his fantasy of an afternoon dance to show what he imagined American life to be, when he was a child.

A dream dance

De Mejo did something special to make this painting look dream-like. He repeated many things to make patterns or designs: look at the patterns made by the teapots, cups and glasses on the table. The shadows of the people and the palm trees make another pattern on the ground. Most of the people sitting down are doing exactly the same thing—crossing their legs. The children look like copies of the adults. And the dance itself is a pattern made up of steps that are repeated many times. The little boy at the back of the patio is a self-portrait of the artist as a child.

De Mejo exaggerated the difference in height between the children and the adults.

43

DANCE OF LOVE, 1987
Grimanesa Amoros, Peruvian (born 1962), **acrylic** on canvas, 140 x 115 cm

Grimanesa Amoros grew up in Peru, South America, where she often saw the Inti Festival at Machu Picchu. Wearing large masks and brilliantly coloured costumes decorated with gold, the Quechua peoples celebrated the life-giving power of the sun god. The Indians' contact with the spirit world made a strong impression on Amoros, and colourful images of their rituals became part of her world.

When she went to art school, Amoros was asked to draw human figures and to make them look real. Instead, huge, magical people took over the pages of her drawing pad. Amoros' teacher often scolded her for not following instructions but, knowing that she could make realistic drawings, he was not too harsh.

The painter at work

Amoros uses acrylic paints and large brushes to build up thick layers of clean, quick-drying colours. She always has a vision when she begins, and she paints rapidly, before the spell is broken. In *Dance of Love*, Amoros represented her feelings about life and love. With pale, airy colours and bold, powerful shapes, she painted a boy and girl gliding across the terrace of an enchanted garden.

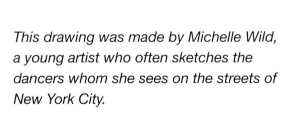

This drawing was made by Michelle Wild, a young artist who often sketches the dancers whom she sees on the streets of New York City.

44

Glossary and Index

ACRYLIC PAINT: **pigment** is combined with an artificial substance called acrylic that is created in a laboratory. By itself, acrylic dries rapidly.

ARCHITECTURE: (1) a building that has been carefully designed and constructed. (2) The art of designing buildings.

BLOTTING PAPER: a soft paper that is used to absorb liquid, particularly ink and oil.

BRITCHES: trousers which go down to the knee or just below. They are usually worn for riding.

CANVAS: a woven fabric (often linen or cotton) used as a painting surface. It is usually stretched tight and stapled on to a wooden frame in order to produce a flat, unwrinkled surface.

CHARCOAL: a soft, black stick of burned wood, used to make drawings. Painters use charcoal because it can be blended and smudged, producing lines and tones of grey.

CHIHIL SITIN: in the Farsi language, it means 'The Hall of Forty Columns'. A pavilion built by Shah Abbas in 1660 next to his palace in Isfahan, Iran (then called Persia); it was used for official dinners and receptions.

FRESCO: a method of painting on to wet plaster, usually with water-colour, to create a picture in which the paint is absorbed into the wall instead of remaining on the surface.

GLAZE: a **transparent**, or almost transparent, thinned-down layer of paint applied over dry paint, allowing the colours underneath to show through.

GOLD LEAF: squares of real gold, pounded thinner than paper. Gold leaf is placed on to a surface coated with tacky glue and carefully pressed into position with soft cotton.

GOUACHE: this is an **opaque** form of **water-colour** paint, which is also called **tempera** or body colour.

INDUSTRIAL REVOLUTION: a period from the late 17th century to the 19th century where work changed from individual labour to labour in factories, mass producing goods such as coal, steel, iron and cloth.

INK: usually, a jet-black fluid. Ink drawings can be made with dark lines and thinned tones of grey. Inks are also made in colours and used in paintings.

MURAL: a very large painting that decorates a wall or is created as part of a wall.

OIL PAINT: pigment, the material used to give paint colour, is mixed with oil (usually linseed or poppy oil). Oil paint is never mixed with water. It is thinned and washed off brushes with turpentine. Oils dry slowly, enabling the artist to work on the painting for a long time. Oil paint has been used since the fifteenth century.

OPAQUE: not letting light pass through. Opaque paints conceal what is under them. (The opposite of **transparent**.)

PASTEL: (1) a soft crayon made from powdered pigment, chalk, water and mixed with a small amount of gum. (2) A painting or sketch made with this type of crayon.

PIGMENT: the raw material that gives paint its colour. It can be made from natural or artificial minerals.

PRIMITIVE: a type of art that is untrained and simple.

ROARING TWENTIES: the 1920s were years of prosperity and celebration after the horrors of World War I.

SILHOUETTES: the dark, usually black, outlined shape of a figure or face.

TEMPERA: **pigment** is combined with raw egg yolk to turn it into a thick paste that can be applied with a brush. Tempera can be washed away with water. Tempera was used by the ancient Greeks and was the favourite method of painters during the medieval period in Europe.

TRANSPARENT: allowing light to pass through so colours underneath can be seen. (The opposite to **opaque**.)

TURPENTINE: a strong-smelling liquid made from pine sap, used in oil painting. *See also* **oil paint**.

WATER-COLOUR: **pigment** is combined with a water-based substance. Water-colour paint is thinned with water and areas of paper are often left uncovered to produce highlights. Water-colour paint was first used 37,000 years ago by cave dwellers who created the first wall paintings.

Credits